For Jo[...]

YOUR WORDS HAVE
INSPIRED ME & I HOPE
THESE WORDS CAN
DO THE SAME FOR
YOU

A WARRIOR
AND A
POET

Principles & Poems

JASON A. HENDERSON

authorHOUSE®

AuthorHouse™
1663 Liberty Drive
Bloomington, IN 47403
www.authorhouse.com
Phone: 833-262-8899

Published by AuthorHouse   07/11/2022

ISBN: 978-1-6655-6451-9 (sc)
ISBN: 978-1-6655-6449-6 (hc)
ISBN: 978-1-6655-6450-2 (e)

Library of Congress Control Number: 2022912944

Print information available on the last page.

This book is printed on acid-free paper.

PROLOGUE

A manuscript about short quotes of principles and poems to guide and inspire in life: I served in United States Navy as a Fleet Marine Force Hospital Corpsman during my time in the military. At any given time, I may be responsible for the health and well-being of a hundred or more of the nation's toughest warfighters, the United States Marines. While deploying with them to various locations, I learned that not all wounds are visible, and sometimes you need someone to hear or speak to you. So I started this as a way to keep my marines up through inspirational words of poems and imagery. I learned that a warrior could be a poet, and a poet could be a warrior, but the key was understanding not to hide from one but to embrace both was the key to keeping my marines going. So I thought it best to put this out there. I hope it finds that person who can benefit from embracing the world or its experiences that come from both.

"The belief in oneself starts with one in the mirror before anyone else believes. The one in the mirror must believe so everyone else will. Be your own biggest fan and the bandwagon will follow"

–Jason Henderson

"Whatever it takes
grind through the Grit,
for the Grit paves the way
to your kingdom of success.
For every kingdom
has a gritty story"

-Jason Henderson

"There is no competition its just me versus me everyone else was just practice"

–Jason Henderson

"What is it to task me with building a road from the person who demands moving the heavens and mountains of oneself"

-Jason Henderson

"My standards for me are higher than their greatest expectations, So I set forth to shatter all records and be the bar that they aspire to be, the standard they will be compared to"

-Jason Henderson

"It cant rain forever the sun will come and the storm will pass so keep my head up and my eyes open opportunities on the horizon"

-Jason Henderson

"My Life is shattered dreams,
Pieced back together are opportunities of new means
The real key to life adapt,
To evolve no problem will ever leave you trapped"

-Jason Henderson

"When I make a plan I depend on me, myself, and I. The only ones I can ever truly hold accountable for actions and attitude in the situation"

-Jason Henderson

"Friends are ones I don't have to compartmentalize, I can break bread with at my last supper"

-Jason Henderson

"Good People + Good Times = Great Memories"

-Jason Henderson

"A new day,
a new chance
for new opportunity"

–Jason Henderson

"Im not bound by yesterday,
Im not afraid of tomorrow,
Im not going to forget to embrace today"

–Jason Henderson

"Every mistake is success waiting to happen"

-Jason Henderson

"I Make my own Destiny, you can always change your situation, let fate follow you as you pave the uncharted road"

-Jason Henderson

Pain is temporary,
Scars are cool,
Pride is forever,
Be great or die great

-Jason Henderson

"101 reasons not one damn excuse"

-Jason Henderson

"No excuse, why are you reading this, get it done"

-Jason Henderson

"Do something because anything is better than nothing"

-Jason Henderson

"A man that stands for nothing cannot be something"

-Jason Henderson

"To bare the cross of being great you have to be willing to the weight"
-Jason Henderson

"Never give up because you are closer than you know, the moment you feel it's the hardest is toward the end. Turn the finish line to your starting point and your mind will see you through it"

-Jason Henderson

"Your current position does not define your abilities nor your intelligence to achieve your desired goal"

-Jason Henderson

"Life is to short to live in fear, but if your going to have a fear of it, then fear not enjoying and appreciating each moment like it was your last"

-Jason Henderson

"When you know what is wrong, you can help to make it right"

-Jason Henderson

"I do not fear death for I have lived and loved in life"

-Jason Henderson

"The question isn't if you can take a bullet, its can you withstand the entire clip"

-Jason Henderson

"Preparation is the biggest and first step you can take towards success"
-Jason Henderson

"You learn to work with the people you hate and play with the people you love"

-Jason Henderson

"Just because you see snow where you are, doesn't mean the world isn't getting warmer. See the bigger picture beyond your own horizon."

–Jason Henderson

"When things go wrong as sometimes they will,
When the road you're trudging seems all up hill,
When funds are low and debts are high,
you want to smile but you have to sigh,
When care is pressing you down a bit,
Rest if you must but don't you quit,
Life is queer with twists and turns,
As every one of us sometimes learns,
And many a failure turns about,
When he might have won had he stuck it out,
Don't give up though the pace seems slow,
You may succeed with another blow,
success is failure turned inside out,
The silver tint of the clouds of doubt,
And you never can tell how close you are,
It may be near when it seems so far,
So stick to the fight when your hardest hit,
Its when things seem worst that you must not quit"

—Unknown

"THUG

True Hero Under God"

–Jason Henderson

"There can be no fate but what I make"

-Jason Henderson

"I fight
with the devil
not to win
but to show the beast
there is no fear
or temptation
for men
who
have already conquered
their own heart
and mind.
There is room
For
only one conquer
and I am it"

–Jason Henderson

"Sometimes the only way to advance is burn your only way of refuge or retreat"

-Jason Henderson

"Fear is a weapon more powerful than any bomb. Control it and control the hearts of men"

-Jason Henderson

"If given only one opportunity would you rather be feared or loved? Being loved depends on others feelings toward you. Being feared depends on your feeling about yourself"

-Jason Henderson

"Respect by fear,
fear by respect
Either brings respect"

– Jason Henderson

"Those that are ruled by their own appetite will always be ruled by their enemy"

-Jason Henderson

"To be loved others control your situation. To be feared means you control their situation. Think one sniper versus an entire 100 man unit. The fear causes the 100 men's movements to be dictated by one man"

-Jason Henderson

"Don't waste time being shy. Time will come and go as it pleases"

-Jason Henderson

"You get respect by both leading and doing, not by mindless following"
-Jason Henderson

"You don't know what you don't know, your imagination can only stretch as far as your knowledge. So read more, learn more, experience more, and you don't have to worry about overloading your brain"

-Jason Henderson

"Will Smith said, "Danger is real, Fear is a choice"; so choose not to be in fear. Understand the danger but choose not to let it hinder your journey. That's courage!"

–Will Smith, Jason Henderson

"For What you are I will be more"
For what you fear
will conquer
For what you despise
I will love,
For what you don't understand
I will learn,
For that I will always be
what you cant

                                                    -Jason Henderson

"The greatest deception is to make people believe there is no deception"
-Jason Henderson

THE STROM

"Hurricane,
I am the storm,
I can choose to be swept out,
into the sea of life no longer to exist,
or I can reshape the world around me,
like the magnificent storm I am"

-Jason Henderson

"A distinction without a difference still yields the same result. Which is quietly mistaken for progression when there is regression"

–Jason Henderson

"Cautious of danger is not the same as timid from fear"

-Jason Henderson

"We burn the bridge behind us because on this day we came to die or conquer"

-Jason Henderson

"Two greatest things you can ever give me is time and information, for both are priceless. Once given it can never be taken back"

-Jason Henderson

"Its hard for you to understand what you don't know. Because your imagination only stretches as far as your knowledge. Making you only able to conceive thoughts of imagination built upon the foundation of the knowledge you have and unable to comprehend what's beyond this. So increase your knowledge to increase your imagination"

-Jason Henderson

"A habit of excellence is a life time of discipline"

-Jason Henderson

"If attitude is the difference between failure and the success then shouldn't we change our attitude toward the problem"

-Jason Henderson

"There is no problem just your attitude toward the given situation"
–Jason Henderson

"Your perception is reality. So perceive yourself to be better than you were yesterday, and greater than you were tomorrow, then today you will always be at your best"

-Jason Henderson

"There is more truth in what's chosen not to be said,
than what is said.
Learn to listen to the silence
and it will speak truth.
I know more about you
because of what you don't say
and how you act,
then what you do say
and try to portray"

-Jason Henderson

"Impossible is not fact its opinion, therefore irrelevant among accomplishments"

-Jason Henderson

"If a man wont treat you right he wont teach you right, question every motive but judge him not by his kind words but by actions"

-Jason Henderson

"Your passion of life should be your alarm clock"

-Jason Henderson

"You only begin to live life
when you become a collector
of not materials
but memories"

–Jason Henderson

"Oppression is obtained
through remaining peaceful.
Liberty and freedom
are obtained through forceful resistance"

-Jason Henderson

"Hope is not a strategy, it's a declaration for a better plan and its application"

-Jason Henderson

"Faith is not a solution it's a byproduct of discipline and conviction to follow through with what you believe in"

-Jason Henderson

"There is no failure until you discontinue your stride for success. Let each breath be affirmation for continuation within that stride"

-Jason Henderson

"WHAT I DON'T KNOW"

You don't know
what you don't know,
until you ask questions.
How can you know
what your doing
is right
or wrong
until it's questioned.
So never
stop
asking questions.

-Jason Henderson

"The road to enlightenment is a bridge paved over those who do not question"

-Jason Henderson

To live in a moment
letting all inhibition go
is ecstasy, simplicity, and true freedom.
Few will ever experience

                                        -Jason Henderson

"Time is the deciding factor it can either make you or break you, so the question to always ask is what will I do better"

-Jason Henderson

Speak it in to existence,
learn from it,
Speak it in to existence,
grow from it,
Speak it into existence,
evolve from it.
Speak it in to existence,
manifest destiny truly I'm it

-Jason Henderson

"Speed kills, strength punishes, I'm both so call me capital punishment"
-Jason Henderson

"Oppression is obtained through remaining peacefully silent; Liberty, justice and freedom are obtained through forceful resistance"

-Jason Henderson

"I think that in order for one to see the truth so clearly, you must turn the mirror on both yourself and the world. As well as possess both a telescope and reading glasses to see the big picture as well the fine intricacy of life and the world"

–Jason Henderson

"Its not the climb or the obstacles that define you its your response and approach to the adversity. You are the change you seek to be or the stubborn rock you choose not to move"

-Jason Henderson

"If people wont save a life out of good common decency. Then appeal to their wallets. Everyone loses money when your patrons to scared to come in or too dead to spend money. Even stray bullets have to find customers"

-Jason Henderson

"you don't need a plan B when your plan A can adapt"

-Jason Henderson

"Do not worry about failure or the next plan when your objective is success and the goal is the destination. So just press forward without hesitation"
-Jason Henderson

"I'd rather a honest enemy close than a false friend"

-Jason Henderson

"Its easier to trick someone of a falsehood than it is to convince them of the truth. Only a fool thinks they have not been fooled"

-Jason Henderson

"GRAB YOUR GAS MASK"

Gas, Gas, Gas
Always have your gas mask.
Because no matter how many guns
and bullets you have
the enemy can surprise you
with a gas attack.
You can never be prepared,
never under estimate your enemy
or the situation.
The universe
may roll in your enemies favor
but when your prepared it will always be in your favor

—Jason Henderson

"When success is all your rhetoric or the only vocabulary you will allow, failure is not known nor will it be presented to you as an option"

-Jason Henderson

"you have a responsibility to find the truth let this be your only absolute and you will always be righteous in your actions"

-Jason Henderson

"There are only two things in this existence that can stop you, You if you give up and two if you die. So I wont stop being successful until I die"

-Jason Henderson

"Success deems that you stop worrying about the perfect and not be intimidated by the what-if scenario. Because sometimes the imperfect is better than the perfect"

-Jason Henderson

"You can trade hours for dollars or ideas for millions"

-Jason Henderson

"Its nothing wrong with having fear. But it takes courage to face it. Fear must be beaten into submission by sheer will. For the only thing fear respects is those that have the courage to face it, will to see it through.

Perseverance through dedication = Will

Discipline of focus through adversity =courage

$$\frac{FEAR}{WILL + COURAGE} = SUCCESS"$$

-Jason Henderson

"Simply WILL + COURAGE = NO FEAR"

-Jason Henderson

"If there was ever a day to be pessimistic is when you die, the time to be optimistic everyday your alive"

-Jason Henderson

"The failure of a pessimist is their not as smart as they would like to believe they are. The success of an optimist is they don't know how smart they really are. So they only see each situation as a chance to learn, grow, and develop into more than what they were. Capitalizing on every created opportunity is the humble dummy"

–Jason Henderson

"Difficult doesn't scare me, it doesn't stop me, its just an excuse for me to do it and succeed"

-Jason Henderson

"Why you must fight, because peace is not an option until your willing to fight for it, sweat for it, bleed for it, and committed enough to die for it"

-Jason Henderson

Using your handicap to your advantage,
is the mark of a true survivalist.
Adapt and overcome.
Because you have no wings to fly
you learn to be a great swimmer
crossing seas and oceans.
Using your handicap to your advantage,
is the mark of a true survivalist.
Adapt and overcome.
Because your movements weren't fast like the cheetah
or swift like the impala,
you become clever like the fox to set traps eating better than both
Using your handicap to your advantage,
is the mark of a true survivalist.
Adapt and overcome.

-Jason Henderson

"Average work week

24hours X 7days = 168hours per week

$$- \left(\begin{array}{l} \text{8work hours X 5days = 40 hours per week} \\ \text{- + 8sleep hours X 7days = 56 hours of sleep per week} \end{array} \right)$$

72 Free hours

What are you doing with your 72"

-Jason Henderson

"Small moments can have a monumental impact, 72 free tick tocks you got it"

-Jason Henderson

"A line can be defined as a straight path from one point to another point. But life is defined by all the things in between. Enjoy these moments in life, instead of things being problems they are stepping stones to make you better for your next destination"

-Jason Henderson

"Its not enough to tell the truth. Tell the truth the audience needs to hear the way they need to hear it"

-Jason Henderson

"FOR YOU"

Give yourself what you wish
you could get from someone else.
If its love
then love yourself,
if its respect then
respect yourself,
if its joy
then enjoy the moments with yourself,
if its admiration
then take pride in all that you do.
For this no one can break you.
Only you can make you

-Jason Henderson

"Don't Fall victim to the smoke and mirrors that keep you waiting for miracles to change your life. You're the only miracle needed to make a change"

-Jason Henderson

"Justice is not blind nor ignorant.
It is an edged sword
that goes to whomever
willing to take it and use it"

–Jason Henderson

"When your mind says it has reached your limits and you crash into that wall of discomfort that's when its time to fight through the grit and start"
-Jason Henderson

"Its too hard to figure out how to give up. So I just accomplish my goals"
-Jason Henderson

"The Stride"
There is no failure
until you discontinue your stride
for success.
Let each Breath
be Affirmation for
confirmation
within that stride

-Jason Henderson

"Peace"
Serenity,
Heaven
Is a place
Found not up,
Nor down,
Left
Or
Right,
But
The mind
And Heart

–Jason Henderson

"WHY HOPE AND FAITH ARE FRIENDS"

Hope is not a strategy
It's a declaration
For a better plan
And its application

Faith is not a solution
It's a byproduct
For discipline with conviction
To follow-through
What you believe in

Hope is not a strategy
It's a declaration
For a better plan
And its application

Faith is not a resolution
But a byproduct
Of obedience in actions
Toward your conviction

Hope is not a strategy
It's a declaration
For a better plan
And its application

Faith is not absolution
It's a byproduct
For foundation of success
From the labor of your fruit

-Jason Henderson

"Godspeed til we meet again"
Tis not night
But day be upon ye!
A light will soon be known,
Tame the untamed,
Claim the unclaimed,
Conquer the unconquered,
Reach for that to be said,
To be to far to be reached,
So let life be ye journey,
Filled wit challenges be surpassed,
For when thy hands put on the stars,
For only thy mind to trap the behind bars,
Sail the seven seas or if it be oceans,
Let the bare heel touch every continent,
As ur journey take ye where be content,
Tis not a good bye, farewell, or adieu,
Just Godspeed til we r face to face again!

-Jason Henderson

"A PATRIOTS REQUEST" **********

A sun has three stages, A rise, peak, and, fall.
Let our country resemble a Sunrise, When the day is full of promise.
Our country needs to stand united,
As the model to the rest of the world, a nation full of promise.

For a country at its peak is on the verge of falling.
While it shines the brightest and burns with much vigor
A country at its height much like gravity or empires past all have fallen.
Waiting for sunset and dark times while still bright and full of vigor

A country on its sunset
Has seen its last good days
As it prepares for dark times.
A country at its peak,
Has already seen its best the day
Has to offer, the promise of a better day has all but pass.
As they sit on the twilight of everything that could have, is now, and
will never be.
They to will wait
As those like the sunset,
Which inevitably bring dark times.
Let our country resemble the sunrise when the day is most beautiful
and full of promise.
When there seems no end
To what could, what is, and what will,
Our country needs to stand united
As the model to the rest of the world.
A nation full of hope, life, and promise.
"Before the Wall"
I wish I could have met you back in time,
Back when sweet words sounded with a touch of sublime,

Before when you only receive gifts to amend actions taken a sour,
A day there was no fear sharing your feelings well in to late hour,
That period in life no construction for the Great Wall,
When it would be so easy to text but you rather a call,

I wish I would have met you back in time,
Before every sweet word was soured by lime,
Before every flower came with thorns of pain for its price,
A prelude to a day when all men weren't a bad roll of the dice,
I can tell you this or that while being O'so charming,
Yet in your head past tears and scars make it much more alarming,

I wish I should have met you way back in time,
Back then speaking sweet words to you wasn't crime,
Before actions of adulation were gestures of spoil,
A moment in time adored being treated as royal,
That point in life put no distance between us,
If I crossed the ocean you would meet me plane, train, or bus

-Jason Henderson

Change comes through strength.
      Peace
comes through War

-Jason Henderson

"Making success convenient is the key to sustained success. Surround yourself with things that make positive habits that move you forward towards the goal"

-Jason Henderson

How to stay motivated?
    Just start
Be consistent
    Just Finish

-Jason Henderson

"IBIZA SUNSET"

I know your day will be filled with wonderful things
such a glow better than diamond rings
from your head to your feat
just a wonderful treat
time seems to not sit still
life with you quite a deal
waking up to you is a sunrise
a daily joy gazing those your are to my eyes
Ibiza magic where we met
Ibiza brought you My Beautiful Sunset

-Jason Henderson

BEAUTIFUL SUNSET

I call you "Beautiful Sunset"
because you are a reflection
of all the beautiful energy
you put out and the excitement
for what you will bring tomorrow.
If I had to wait a whole day
a whole year
for the moment
that you reflect your beautiful ways
it would be a lifetime worth waiting
even for just one of those days!

-Jason Henderson

"DISTANT HEART"

Unattainable Heart
Im everything she needs but nothing she wants
She seeks comfort in one's that would break her heart
She runs from comfort of strong stable arms
To those of a shaky forever wavering hands
She finds joy in those that would leave her in shambles
Instead of the man that would pick her up
She's happy with the one that covers a lie within a joke
The one that would give her the world if she ask she despise
Forever to the earnest she remains just another unattainable heart

-Jason Henderson

"REAL LOVE IS WHAT YOU BREATHE"

Real Love is what you breathe
You have been holding your breath for a life time.
Your body is tired and your waiting to let go
and exhale.
Im that first breath of fresh air
filling your body expanding your lungs,
and revitalizing your mind.
Putting you at ease
giving you the stability and security
that all will continue to be well.
Each breath gets sweeter and full,
my love is life,
the first real breath you take.

–Jason Henderson

It doesn't matter if someone is smarter than you or stronger than you. If you get the information you can act first. Giving you the advantage that can neutralize your adversary before they can even get started.

-Jason Henderson

There is only two ways a man can be defeated. Either you die or quit. So die trying rather than quit. So I will either die or be successful. Life is that simple.

-Jason Henderson

WARRIORS LETTER TO A FATHER/MOTHER

Victory may come on the heels of my death
Yield not to despair for I met every challenge
With courage and even my end I would with joy no remorse
For a life fulfilled
Is a life well lived
Though you do not know my brothers
Not bond by blood but by conviction
To shed blood for the same cause
Honor, Duty, Integrity
These are my Countrymen

For God
For Family
For Country

You Raised a warrior
This Warrior salutes you

For those who no longer here to see a sunrise
I will continue the March before the Dawn
For days past and holidays missed
Know it was for duty to fight the good fight
Should a bright light be at the end of this tunnel.

-Jason Henderson

I GO TO WAR

To Battle I Ride
Day or Night
To Battle I Ride
Never waiver to Fight
To Battle I Ride
Through Ice and Fire
To Battle I Ride
To forge or break an empire

So again I say

To Battle I Ride
Neither death nor impalement yield the march
To Battle I Ride
Blood spilled plentiful like red cornstarch
To Battle I Ride
Despite the danger courageous remains the heart
To Battle I Ride
Adaptability over stratagem wins the part

So Again I say

To Battle I Ride
Even out numbered and surrounded by the adversary
To Battle I ride
The Warrior fights to see sunrise over the prairie
To Battle I Ride
For the warrior peace is found in the unrest
To Battle I ride
Fate shall collect in blood he who is not at his best

-Jason Henderson

WARRIORS PRAYER

Before War I see Heaven but I feel Hell
I hear the wings of the helios
I feel the drums of war
I smell the tears of the fallen

I ask you Heavenly father for the Will to Keep going
I ask you for the wits to a little wiser than the fox
I ask you for the strength to be a little stronger than the Ox
I ask you for the quickness to be a little quicker than a gazelle

Before War I see Heaven but I feel Hell
I hear the wings of the helios
I feel the drums of war
I smell the tears of the fallen
I ask you let thy hand be as steady of a tailor as he threads through a
needle may move with no fault
I ask you let my eyes be that of an eagle missing no level of earth as I
look for the smallest of infractions
I ask you give me the compassion like a new parent so that I may send
my enemies mercy swiftly
I ask that you make me like a clock so I may be timely so I may arrange
my enemies to meet you on time
    AMEN

-Jason Henderson

FOR YOU OUR LOVE I WOULD

For You I would move mountains
     And part the seas,
Our love is the sweetest of things
     Said even by Honey Bees,
I would climb the highest of peaks
     Go the deepest of depth,
A love this deep is like emerging for fresh air
     Filling lungs at its widest breadth,
Even with the furthest stars just out of reach
     If its desired I'll have them yours,
This love so warm like a summer Ibiza Sunset
     On the beach cooking cacao smores,

For you I would give you the best of the world
     Even if only for Gelato and Ice cream,
Our love is that once in a lifetime thing
     So I will love you wake or dream,
I would go to the infinity and beyond
     So nothing need be ask by you,
A day of its best or its worst
     Always better just us too,
Even with you being so distant at Venus
     Be there in no time from Mars,
This love burns more stronger than the sun
     Brighter than night lit stars,

For you I would see it out until the end
     Even through fire and Ice,
Our days while not always, yet far and few could get bad
     Life with you nothing more nice,
I would tell you a truth I love you, I love you, I love you
     For this I cannot spend life being to coy,

A eternity I could spend forever in smiles
      Because even a day I was your joy,
Even if I had to give my life the ultimate sacrifice
      For you there's no need to bet,
This love so deep its just to sit with each other divine ecstasy
      Bliss as we cross arms gazing another sunset

                       –Jason Henderson

LOVE

Loyalty
   Open-hearted
     Value
       Embrace

-Jason Henderson

GHOST OF FREEDOM

I have spent a life time defending this country
For people who will never know me
I sacrificed my freedoms so you could have them
To my brothers and sisters at arms
We work in the dark
You will not know my name
Because of my profession I cannot have fame
At zero dark thirty we go to work
Bad guy after bad guy we make disappear
So you can dream safe in the clear
The job rarely comes with a thanks
Discipline remains when in danger we file in ranks
My team will remain as midnight ghost
So this will be their only acknowledgment post

-Jason Henderson

FAREWELL

I will speak in a breviloquent manner where I will you send off...

A farewell this can surely not be,
Tis not night but day that be upon us,
Tis not a shadow of the unknown,
For it , a light t'will soon known

Dread no, for t'was not of learned,
So ye chord may embrace,
in which shall be learned.

For thou shall chart what has been uncharted,
Discover the undiscovered, tame the untamed,

Let ye put our feet on the sky,
and our hands on the stars,
For nothing not be ascertainable,
Les ye all but reach toward thy desire.

For our walk together be at a twilight,
So to you Adieu, I dare not, I fair not,
Nor will a farewell be of a due,
Shall to our fates path entwine.

For thou look upon thy day of glee,
Rich hopeful eyes, of nay myopic heart thy guide,
Tis a joined past given savory recall,
Til thy memoir of then be but filled,
One word to lead thy journey, to all I say
Godspeed...

-Jason Henderson